Caring for Widows

by
John MacArthur, Jr.

"GRACE TO YOU"
P.O. Box 4000
Panorama City, CA   91412

ISBN: 0-8024-5326-0

1 2 3 4 5 Printing/LC/Year 95 94 93 92 91

Printed in the United States of America

Contents

These Bible studies are taken from messages delivered by Pastor-Teacher John MacArthur, Jr., at Grace Community Church in Sun Valley, California. These messages have been combined into a 4-tape album titled *Caring for Widows*. You may purchase this series either in an attractive vinyl cassette album or as individual cassettes. To purchase these tapes, request the album *Caring for Widows*, or ask for the tapes by their individual GC numbers. Please consult the current price list; then send your order, making your check payable to:

"GRACE TO YOU"
P.O. Box 4000
Panorama City, CA 91412

Or call the following toll-free number:
1-800-55-GRACE

1

Widows in the Church—Part 1

Outline

Introduction
A. Old Testament Teaching
B. New Testament Teaching
　1. The example of Christ
　　a) In the Temple
　　b) In a widow's home
　　c) On the cross
　2. The example of the early church
　　a) The church at Jerusalem
　　b) Peter at Joppa

Lesson
I. The Church's Obligation to Support Widows (v. 3)
　A. Defining *Widows*
　B. Honoring Widows
　C. Supporting Widows
II. The Church's Obligation to Evaluate their Needs (vv. 4-8)
　A. Widows with Families (v. 4)

Conclusion

Introduction

By God's design, a wife is to be the special object of her husband's love and care. As "a weaker vessel" (1 Pet. 3:7), she is under his authority and protection. But if a woman loses her husband, she is often left without any means of financial support. Such women are under God's special care. The psalmist said the Lord is "a defender of widows" (Ps. 68:5, NIV*; cf. Deut. 10:18). God's compassion goes out to them because of their difficult situation. And Scripture reveals that has always been God's attitude toward widows.

A. Old Testament Teaching

1. Deuteronomy 27:19—"Cursed be he who perverteth the justice due . . . the . . . widow."

2. Isaiah 1:17—"Plead for the widow."

3. Jeremiah 22:3-4—"Do no violence to the . . . widow. . . . For if ye do this thing indeed, then shall there enter in by the gates of this house kings sitting upon the throne of David . . . he, and his servants, and his people."

4. Exodus 22:22-23—"Ye shall not afflict any widow. . . . If thou afflict them in any way, and they cry at all unto me, I will surely hear their cry."

God blessed those who cared for widows but cursed those who didn't. The Old Testament also taught that remarriage was the ideal for a widow. Where remarriage was not possible, a widow could stay either in the house of her parents (cf. Gen. 38:11) or in-laws (cf. Ruth 1:16). And according to Levirate marriage (Deut. 25:5-6), the brother of the deceased husband could marry her. If he refused, the next male-of-kin was free to do so. Boaz married Ruth in that manner (Ruth 4:1-10).

B. New Testament Teaching

1. The example of Christ

New International Version.

a) In the Temple

Jesus Christ exemplified the perfect attitude toward widows. Mark 12 tells us that Jesus sat opposite the Temple treasury as worshipers gave their money offerings. He noticed that the wealthy gave large amounts of money but that a widow gave only a small amount. Jesus said to His disciples, "This poor widow hath cast more in than all they who have cast into the treasury; for all they did cast in of their abundance, but she of her want did cast in all that she had, even all her living" (vv. 43-44). Christ commended the widow's worship. Her generous spirit was evidence that she had a sincere and godly heart.

b) In a widow's home

As Jesus approached the city of Nain, "there was a dead man carried out, the only son of his mother, and she was a widow, and many people of the city were with her" (Luke 7:12). Because of her son's death, no one was left to care for her. When the Lord saw her, He "had compassion on her, and said unto her, Weep not. And he came and touched the bier; and they that bore him sat still. And he said, Young man, I say unto thee, Arise. And he that was dead sat up, and began to speak. And he delivered him to his mother" (vv. 13-15). Jesus was so touched by the widow's plight that He raised her son from the dead so he could continue to care for her.

c) On the cross

John 19 tells us that when Jesus, hanging on the cross, "saw his mother, and the disciple standing by, whom he loved, he saith unto his mother, Woman, behold thy son! Then saith he to the disciple, Behold thy mother! And from that hour that disciple took her unto his own home" (vv. 26-27). Jesus deeply cared about Mary, so He entrusted her to the apostle John's care.

9

2. The example of the early church

  a) The church at Jerusalem

     Because of its rapid numerical growth "there arose
     a murmuring of the Grecians against the Hebrews,
     because their widows were neglected in the daily
     ministration" (Acts 6:1). "Hebrews" refers to Jewish
     people living in Palestine whereas "Grecians" (also
     called Hellenists) refers to Jewish people who had
     been dispersed or scattered outside of Palestine.
     Hellenists came to Jerusalem for holidays, and
     some even moved to Palestine to live. Perhaps
     those referred to in Acts 6 were residents of the
     city, or stayed in homes with other Christian fam-
     ilies, or were housed at various inns.

     Apparently the Hellenistic widows in the church
     did not receive the same care as those from Pal-
     estine. Perhaps that was because the Hellenistic
     people were not a part of the original Jewish com-
     munity. Whatever the reason, the apostles gathered
     the believers together and asked them to find "sev-
     en men of honest report, full of the Holy Spirit
     and wisdom" to care for the Hellenistic widows
     (v. 3). Honesty was necessary since they would be
     handling money and food; wisdom and the Spirit's
     control were necessary to evaluate each widow's
     need with sensitivity. The plan pleased the Hellenis-
     tic believers, and seven such men were chosen.

  b) Peter at Joppa

     In the city of Joppa lived a kind and gracious be-
     liever named Tabitha (also called Dorcas), but she
     became sick and died (Acts 9:36-37). Normally it
     was not the Jewish custom to embalm the body but
     only to wash it for a time of viewing or mourning
     (v. 37).

     The believers in Joppa heard that Peter was in the
     nearby city of Lydda, so they sent for him, ob-
     viously knowing he had demonstrated the power
     of God through many previous miracles. Perhaps

they hoped he could do something for Tabitha as well. So Peter journeyed there and came to the room where she lay. "All the widows stood by him weeping, and showing the coats and garments which Dorcas had made, while she was with them" (v. 39). Dorcas had apparently used her own resources to make clothing for a number of destitute widows.

Then Peter asked everyone in the room to leave, "kneeled down, and prayed; and turning to the body said, Tabitha, arise. And she opened her eyes; and when she saw Peter, she sat up" (v. 40). There was probably confusion along with the weeping. Peter was considerate in having them leave the room rather than trying to stop their crying. He probably wanted to be alone to pray as well. It was the second resurrection recorded in the New Testament that benefited widows, the first being the resurrection of the widow's son in Nain. The brokenhearted widows of Joppa were comforted because the woman so dear to them had been raised from the dead.

The book of James summarizes God's compassion for widows: "Pure religion and undefiled before God and the Father is this: to visit the fatherless and widows in their affliction, and to keep oneself unspotted from the world" (1:27). A believer demonstrates his faith by deeds of love and mercy to those in need.

Paul wanted the church to demonstrate its faith that way. His lengthy section on widows (1 Tim. 5:3-16) shows the importance of the subject. In that section, he gave several principles to govern the church's conduct toward widows.

Lesson

I. THE CHURCH'S OBLIGATION TO SUPPORT WIDOWS (v. 3)

"Honor widows that are widows indeed."

A. Defining *Widows*

The Greek term translated "widow" (*chēra*) means "bereft" and conveys a sense of suffering loss or being left alone. The term does not tell us how a woman became a widow, and therefore the cause is not limited to a husband's death. "Widows indeed" is qualified by the Greek term translated "desolate" (*ontōs*; v. 5), which means "having been left alone." It indicates that no one is able to help her.

In ancient times, widows were in an especially difficult position because honorable employment for women was not readily available, neither were there any secular institutions to provide for them. Perhaps some could receive help through family or friends, but many lived in poverty, never having received an inheritance. Since the outlook for many was bleak, it was vital for the church to assist them. In fact, as we saw in James 1:27, the treatment of widows was a test whereby believers demonstrated the genuineness of their faith.

B. Honoring Widows

Christian widows left alone are to receive "honor" (Gk., *timaō*, "to revere" or "value"), if they meet the qual-ifications that Paul later mentions.

Matthew 15 illustrates that honor includes financial support. The scribes and Pharisees confronted Jesus, saying, "Why do thy disciples transgress the tradition of the elders?" (v. 2). The "tradition of the elders" was a large compilation of rules and regulations imposed upon the Jewish people's way of life. It developed from interpretations of Scripture by various Jewish religious leaders but often added to or even contradicted Scripture.

The scribes and Pharisees said Christ's disciples violated their tradition because they "wash not their hands when they eat bread" (v. 2). That washing had nothing to do with sanitation but was directly related to a religious, ceremonial cleansing.

Since the disciples didn't recognize the tradition as scriptural, they simply ignored it. And Jesus responded by saying, "Why do ye also transgress the commandment of God by your tradition? For God commanded, saying, Honor thy father and mother; and, He that curseth father or mother, let him die the death. But ye say, Whosoever shall say to his father or his mother, It is a gift, by whatsoever thou mightest be profited by me; and honor not his father or mother, he shall be free. Thus have ye made the commandment of God of no effect by your tradition" (vv. 3-6). His explanation included a reference to the Ten Commandments about honoring your parents (Ex. 20:12). The Jewish people in the days of Moses understood that to include financial support.

But the tradition that developed contradicted the intent of that commandment. It allowed a person to pledge money to God by saying, "It is a gift." The money could then only be given to the Lord. So if a person didn't want to give money to his needy parents, he would simply pledge it to the Lord. If he later decided to keep the money for personal use instead, tradition also allowed him to rescind his original vow. So it served neither God nor family but only selfish interests.

C. Supporting Widows

Widows receiving honor are qualified as "widows indeed." The Greek term translated "indeed" means "in reality" or "in point of fact." The fact is they are alone and therefore in need of financial support. So "widows indeed" are to be distinguished from widows having financial means. Some husbands may have left their wives with wonderful resources such as a home and some money. In those instances, the church should still be there to provide for any spiritual needs.

We live in a country that provides some basic coverage for widows. But the scope of their needs is increasing. Some widows might desire a Christian education for their children, and the church could set up a scholarship fund toward meeting that need. Other widows may have previously lived on a low income while others may have

13

lived on a higher one. So the church will need to exercise wisdom to determine which needs are real ones.

The church must be committed to widows who genuinely need assistance, whatever the cost might be. It may mean transferring money out of optional church programs so basic needs can be met. The church should be happy to do that because it shows God's compassion toward the destitute. Even when widows have financial resources, the church needs to come alongside with encouragement, love, and support in every way possible.

The increasing collapse of the family unit in our society means there will be an increase in the number of widows that need to be under the church's care. For instance, a Christian widow with several children might not receive any help from unsaved parents. It would be good if she could move back into her parents' home (Gen. 38:11), but that is not always possible.

II. THE CHURCH'S OBLIGATION TO EVALUATE THEIR NEEDS (vv. 4-8)

The church needs to discern which widows are in genuine need of financial care. It cannot indiscriminately give to everyone. So Scripture lays down some guidelines to determine who qualifies and who doesn't.

A. Widows with Families (v. 4)

"If any widow have children or nephews, let them learn first to show piety at home, and to requite their parents; for that is good and acceptable before God."

The Greek term translated "nephews" (*ekgonos*) means "descendants" or "grandchildren." Many widows have children and grandchildren. The Greek term translated "home" (*oikos*) refers to the family. "First" indicates a priority of order. Family members are the first ones responsible to care for widows. The first place for children and grandchildren to demonstrate their godliness is in the context of family living, which includes making sure each family member is provided for. In fact, verse 8 says, "If any provide not for his own, and specially for those of his own house, he hath denied the faith, and is worse than an [unbeliever]."

True spirituality reveals itself in the context of family relationships. Paul previously emphasized that in chapter 3, where he said an elder must manage his own household well (v. 4), and a deacon must exercise good oversight over his family (v. 12). The burden isn't only on the older family members: godly young people will desire good relationships with their family members as well. Relating well to each other is an indication of a godly family. Perhaps even an application of enrollment for a seminary student could include a letter of reference from the parents. It might ask, What evidences of godliness have you seen in your child's life?

Family members are not only to show godliness at home but also "to requite" (Gk., *amoibē*, "recompense") their parents. Children are to give back a return to their parents, which includes a financial obligation. Besides providing material items such as food, clothing, and housing, parents also give intangible assets such as love and encouragement. It should be a great and happy privilege for children to return a small measure of the tremendous support they have received from their parents.

Conclusion

A widow in the biblical sense may be a daughter, a mother, a sister, a niece, or an aunt who loses her husband through divorce, desertion, imprisonment, or especially death. Caring for such a woman is a privilege and a manifestation of God's compassion. Paul said doing so "is good and acceptable before God" (v. 4). Parents deserve our respect and support, especially those who are widows.

Focusing on the Facts

1.   Explain the Old Testament teaching about widows (see p. 8).

2. Explain three instances where Christ honored widows (see pp. 8-9).

3. Explain the problem the church at Jerusalem had (Acts 6:1). How did they solve the problem (see p. 10)?

4. Why were the widows at Joppa so sad (Acts 9)? How did Peter comfort them (see pp. 10-11)?

5. What verse summarizes God's compassion for widows (see p. 11)?

6. What is the first principle to guide the church in caring for widows (1 Tim. 5:3; see p. 11)?

7. Explain the meaning of "widows" (1 Tim. 5:3; see p. 12).

8. Why were widows in ancient times often in a difficult financial position (see p. 12)?

9. Define "honor" (1 Tim. 5:3). Give an example of it from Matthew 15:1-6 (see pp. 12-13).

10. Explain the meaning of "indeed" (1 Tim. 5:3; see p. 13).

11. What kind of commitment does the church need to make in caring for widows (see p. 14)?

12. What is the second principle to guide the church in caring for widows (1 Tim. 5:4-8; see p. 14)?

13. Define "nephews" and "home" (1 Tim. 5:4). Who is first obligated to care for widows (see p. 14)?

14. True spirituality reveals itself in the context of _____ _____ (see p. 15).

15. Explain the meaning of "requite" (1 Tim. 5:4; see p. 15).

16. True or false: In the biblical sense a woman becomes a widow only through her husband's death (see p. 15).

17. What is God's evaluation of those who care for widows (1 Tim. 5:4; see p. 15)?

Pondering the Principles

1. Honoring our parents is a duty and privilege (Ex. 20:12; Eph. 6:2). Puritan Richard Baxter said, "Be sure that you dearly love your parents; delight to be in their company; be not like those unnatural children, that love the company of their idle play-fellows better than their parents, and had rather be abroad about their sports, than in their parents' sight. Remember that you have your being from them, and come out of their loins: remember what sorrow you have cost them, and what care they are at for your education and provision; and remember how tenderly they have loved you

. . . and how much your happiness will make them glad: remember what love you owe them both by nature and in justice, for all their love to you, and all that they have done for you: they take your happiness or misery to be one of the greatest parts of the happiness or misery of their own lives" (*The Practical Works of Richard Baxter*, vol. 1 [Ligonier, Pa.: Soli Deo Gloria, 1990], p. 454). Reflect upon the many benefits you have received from your parents. Be sure to express your appreciation to them.

2. True religion involves visiting "widows in their affliction" (James 1:27). *Visiting* speaks of caring for them, and *affliction* refers to anything that burdens or pressures the spirit. Practical deeds of love can help relieve their pressures and burdens. Cleaning their house or taking them with you on trips are simple but important ways to uplift them. Create a list of ways you can help and begin to do them.

2
Widows in the Church—Part 2

Outline

Introduction

Review
I.   The Church's Obligation to Support Widows (v. 3)
II. The Church's Obligation to Evaluate Their Needs (vv. 4-8)
     A. Widows with Families (v. 4)

Lesson
     B. Widows Without Families (vv. 5-6)
        1. Those who qualify for support (v. 5)
           a) Widows who are alone (v. 5a)
           b) Widows who are believers (v. 5b)
           c) Widows who are godly (v. 5c)
        2. Those who don't qualify for support (v. 6)
     C. A Church With a Good Testimony (v. 7)
     D. A Christian With a Bad Testimony (v. 8)
        1. He doesn't show love
        2. He doesn't set a good example

Conclusion

Introduction

Our society will probably continue to see more women with greater needs. That is reflected in George Grant's book, *The Dispossessed: Homelessness in America* (Westchester, Ill.: Crossway, 1986), in which he claims that the feminist movement has been detrimental to the well-being of women, citing several authorities and statistics (pp. 73-79). He uses the phrase *the feminization of poverty* to describe the negative effect the movement has had on women. Economist Sylvia Ann Hewlett makes the same point in her critique, *A Lesser Life: The Myth of Women's Liberation in America*. She says that women have less economic security because of the movement and that it has eroded values such as responsibility, courtesy, respect, and commitment.

Evidence exists to support those claims. The majority of women in the labor force today work out of economic necessity. Most are single, widowed, or divorced and aren't paid as much as men for comparable work. One in three families with women as the head of the household is poor, compared with one in ten of those led by men, and one in nineteen where the home has two parents. Some experts say that, if the trend continues, the poverty population will soon be composed only of women and their children.

Abortion and divorce are directly related to the economic welfare of women. Some women who are poor don't want children, so they abort them. But abortion can cause many medical complications and is now a leading killer in maternal deaths. According to one medical journal, half of the deaths related to abortion are probably not even reported. Even women themselves have become the victims of abortion. As for divorce, Lenore J. Weitzman notes in her book *The Divorce Revolution* that women experience a significant decline in their standard of living in the first year after a divorce, while their former husbands' standard of living increases. Years ago, one out of six American marriages ended in divorce. Today, it is estimated that at least half of current marriages will eventually end in divorce, and demographers expect that statistic to rise.

As the number of women who need help increases, the church will also experience an increased burden. As God's representative to the world, the church should help in the ways it can.

God cares and we should too. One specific group of women in need of its care is widows. So Paul gave the church some principles to go by in caring for them.

Review

I. THE CHURCH'S OBLIGATION TO SUPPORT WIDOWS (v. 3; see pp. 11-14)

II. THE CHURCH'S OBLIGATION TO EVALUATE THEIR NEEDS (vv. 4-8; see pp. 14-15)

A. Widows with Families (v. 4)

Lesson

B. Widows Without Families (vv. 5-6)

Paul stated that widows with families should receive their support from them (v. 4). In verses 5-6 he details how the church should evaluate the needs of those who don't have families. Some widows qualify for support and some don't.

1. Those who qualify for support (v. 5)

   a) Widows who are alone (v. 5a)

   "She that is a widow indeed, and desolate."

   Paul again addresses those who are widows "indeed," who apparently don't have any children or grandchildren willing to care for them (cf. v. 3). The family structure could be missing because of immorality, divorce, abandonment by the children, or even the children's death. The Greek term translated "desolate" (*memonōmevē*) means "has been left alone." We derive the prefix *mono* from it, which means "one," "alone," or "single." The perfect tense indicates a continual condition or state of being. Those women have no one to turn to for help.

b) Widows who are believers (v. 5b)

"Trusteth in God."

The Greek term "trusteth" (*elpizō*) could be translated "she has fixed her hope on God." The perfect tense implies not only a continual condition of being without means, but also a continual at-titude of looking to God as her only hope. That describes a Christian. The Bible says, "Do good unto all men, especially unto them who are of the household of faith" (Gal. 6:10). The church might choose to help non-Christians, but it has a special responsibility to care for its own.

A Christian widow has learned to trust in God as her provider. We see His provision for widows illustrated in 1 Kings 17:8-16. The Lord told Elijah to go to the town of Zarephath. There he would meet a widow who would give him some food and water. When he arrived, he saw a woman gathering together some sticks. He asked her for some water to drink and as she went to get it, he also asked her to bring him a small piece of bread.

But she responded that she had no bread, only a little flour and some cooking oil. She had been gathering the sticks to prepare the last meal for her son and herself. After that, she said they would die. (There was a famine in the land.) Elijah told her to not be afraid but to first make him some bread, and after that, some for themselves because the Lord promised not to allow her supply of flour and oil to be insufficient. So she obeyed, and in fulfilling His promise, God continually provided for her.

c) Widows who are godly (v. 5c)

"Continueth in supplications and prayers night and day."

That speaks of a widow who is committed to God. She entrusts every aspect of her life to Him. Her prayer life is reflective of an intimate relationship with the Lord. "Continueth . . . night and day" indicates a common practice of life. The Greek term translated "supplications" (*deēsesin*) means "to ask" or "entreat." She tells God her needs because she knows He is her provider.

Those are the kinds of widows that the church is to care for. But who is the church? You are! Rather than bringing a needy woman's needs to someone else's attention, first see what you can do.

2. Those who don't qualify for support (v. 6)

"But she that liveth in pleasure is dead while she liveth."

The Greek term translated "but" (*de*) means "on the other hand." This woman lives in contrast to the criteria described in verse 5. "Liveth in pleasure" means "to live luxuriously." Her interest is in a life of ease and self-gratification. The Septuagint describes that kind of person as one who lives in careless ease or unbridled sensuality (e.g., Ezek. 16:49). She may be alive physically, but spiritually she is dead. There's no trust, devotion, or love for God. She lives with disregard for what is right.

The church isn't responsible to support that kind of widow. The implication is that she is to be left to the consequences of her sins, which hopefully will lead her to repent. The church is not obligated to help someone continue a sinful lifestyle.

The context of the verse indicates that there were such women in the church. Maybe a woman was active in the church with her husband, only to leave that lifestyle when she became a widow. Whatever past involvement she may have had with the church, she forsook it. Perhaps her heart was like the rocky soil in which the Word grew until tribulation came, but then died (Matt. 13:20-21). Or possibly her heart was like the weedy ground in which the Word was choked out by the pleasures of the world (Matt. 13:22).

Paul didn't even issue a command—it's obvious that church resources are not for supporting spiritually dead people. That doesn't advance His kingdom.

There are built-in consequences to deviating from God's Word. For example, harmful diseases can result from immorality. Or alcohol can ruin a person's career. The church needs to faithfully teach the Word, which reveals the God who can transform any person's life. People should receive the church's support only when they qualify for it biblically. Those who don't should be left to deal with the consequences of their sin. Hopefully the misery of their sins will lead them to Christ.

C. A Church with a Good Testimony (v. 7)

"These things command, that they may be blameless."

"Things" refers to everything Paul told Timothy since verse 3. Church leaders are to continually instruct the church so that it will maintain an irreproachable testimony. That includes instructing families to fulfill their obligations (vv. 3-4) and widows to live godly lives (vv. 5-6). The church also needs to know which widows qualify to receive its support. So the instruction is to everyone in the church. There will be no cause for criticism when the church cares for widows in the right way.

However, in the name of Christianity, millions of dollars are given to organizations that aren't even centered on the Word of God. Unscrupulous individuals use the money for financial profit, while multitudes struggle to survive. That's wrong! When the unsaved world sees that, they turn away from the church because of the so-called Christian organizations that do such things. So it is important for the church to have a testimony without reproach before God and the world. Its care of widows is directly related to that.

D. A Christian with a Bad Testimony (v. 8)

"But if any provide not for his own, and specially for those of his own house, he hath denied the faith, and is worse than an infidel."

The Greek term translated "but" indicates that verse 8 states negatively what verse 4 says positively: the latter says it's good for families to support their parents; the former says that if they don't they are acting worse than unbelievers.

"Provide" means "think of beforehand" or "care for," indicating that support requires careful forethought and planning. A believer is to support "his own," a general reference to the believer's sphere of relationships. It might be friends, neighbors, acquaintances, or relatives.

"Any" indicates that every believer is responsible to provide that support. When he can, a believer should meet needs without taking it to the organized church. "Specially" means "chiefly" or "most of all." Above all, a Christian is responsible to care for his own family members. If he doesn't care for those God brings into his fold, he is guilty of two things.

1. He doesn't show love

"He hath denied the faith" doesn't refer to someone who has stopped believing in God. Rather, this is someone who is not loving others as he should. That is a serious matter because love is at the center of the Christian faith.

a) John 3:16—"God so loved the world that he *gave*" (emphasis added).

b) Romans 5:5—"The love of God is shed abroad in our hearts."

c) John 13:35—Jesus said, "By this shall all men know that ye are my disciples, if ye have love one to another."

d) 1 Thessalonians 4:9—Paul said, "As touching brotherly love, ye need not that I write unto you; for ye yourselves are taught of God to love one another."

Love will compel you to give sacrificially to others and is the element by which others can tell if you are a Christian (John 17:21-23).

2. He doesn't set a good example

Most unbelievers take care of their own because it's a natural thing to do. They may not understand that doing so is a biblical obligation. And none have Christ to follow as their model or possess His indwelling power. So when a believer doesn't fulfill an obligation that even an unbeliever knows enough to do, he's acting worse than an unbeliever. Even pagans revere and worship their elders and ancestors.

Conclusion

In John 19 Jesus hung on a cross, near death. Gathered at the foot of the cross were His mother; His mother's sister; Mary the wife of Clopas; and Mary Magdalene. Verse 26 says, "When Jesus, therefore, saw his mother, and the disciple standing by, whom he loved, he saith unto his mother, Woman, behold thy son!" Jesus focused her attention on John, not Himself. And John received Mary as his own mother.

Why did Jesus want John to care for her? Joseph already had died, so she had no husband. Now she was losing the Son of her love, the Son of the virgin birth, the Messiah. Apparently Jesus did not want her to be left in the care of His unbelieving brothers. Out of deep love, He responded to her situation so she would receive the proper care.

That tells us something important about caring for widows. As Jesus hung on a cross, He spoke only to two individuals. One was a wretched criminal hanging next to Him, whom He forgave. The other was His widowed mother. Nothing reveals God's heart better than when His Son was dying on a cross to bear the sins of the world. With eternity past and future gathering to a great, redemptive climax, the two things preoccupying His mind were the salvation of a sinner and the care of a widow. Jesus said "woman" (v. 27) and not "mother" probably because He didn't want to make the wound of her heart any deeper. Nor was He to be seen anymore as her son but as her Savior. Although no work was ever more strenuous and inconceivable than what Christ accomplished on the cross, the compassionate heart that beat within our Savior never lost sight of caring for a widow.

Focusing on the Facts

1. Explain the criterion of widows who are alone (1 Tim. 5:5; see pp. 21-22).
2. Explain the criterion of widows who are believers (1 Tim. 5:5; see p. 22).
3. How did the Lord provide for a widow in Zarephath (1 Kings 17:8-16; see p. 22)?
4. Explain the criterion of widows who are godly (1 Tim. 5:5; see pp. 22-23).
5. Who is the church? What is the implication of that (see p. 23)?
6. How do we know that a widow living in pleasure is an unbeliever (1 Tim. 5:6; see p. 23)?
7. Might unsaved widows seek church support? Explain (see pp. 23-24).
8. What does "things" in 1 Timothy 5:7 refer to (see p. 24)?
9. Why is it important for the church to maintain a good testimony (see p. 24)?
10. True or false: The care of widows directly relates to the church's reputation (see p. 24).
11. Explain the significance of "but" at the beginning of 1 Timothy 5:8 (p. 25).
12. Whom does "his own" refer to in 1 Timothy 5:8 (see p. 25)?
13. Explain the significance of "any" in 1 Timothy 5:8 (see p. 25).
14. What does denying the faith as referred to in 1 Timothy 5:8 seem to mean? Support your answer with Scripture (v. 8; see p. 25).
15. How can a Christian act worse than an unbeliever? (1 Tim. 5:8; see p. 26)?

16. Explain how Christ's example on the cross shows the importance of caring for widows (John 19:26; see p. 26).

Pondering the Principles

1. Believers can grow in the faith by learning from the example of a godly Christian widow (1 Tim. 5:5). She has experienced adversity in the loss of her husband and has tasted the bitterness of loneliness. But in her affliction, she still loves God with all her heart, trusting in Him and praying to Him. These are verses she can particularly identify with:

   • Job 23:10-12—"[The Lord] knoweth the way that I take; when he hath tested me, I shall come forth as gold. My foot hath held his steps, his way have I kept, and not declined. Neither have I gone back from the commandment of his lips; I have esteemed the words of his mouth more than my necessary food."

   • Isaiah 26:3—[The Lord] "wilt keep him in perfect peace, whose mind is stayed on thee, because he trusteth in thee."

   • Romans 8:28, 32—"All things work together for good to them that love God" and He "freely [gives] us all things."

   Learn from a Christian who has experienced adversity and yet maintains a godly testimony. If you are presently in a difficult situation, allow God to comfort you through His Word, knowing "that the trial of your faith, being much more precious than of gold that perisheth, though it be tried with fire, might be found unto praise and honor and glory at the appearing of Jesus Christ" (1 Pet. 1:7).

2. First Timothy 5:8 illustrates that love for others is at the center of the Christian faith. John Hooper said, "Love of man necessarily arises out of the love of God. The love of the creature is but the corollary to the love of the Creator. This is what the Christian finds, as a matter of fact. His heart is overcharged with love to God. It finds its way out in love to man" (*The Golden Treasury of Puritan Quotations*, I. D. E.

Thomas, ed. [Edinburgh: The Banner of Truth Trust, 1989], p. 176).

Prayerfully consider the verses below and allow God to give you an awareness of others' needs and an increasing desire to help them.

- Romans 13:8—"Owe no man anything, but to love one another; for he that loveth another hath fulfilled the law."

- Galatians 5:14—"All the law is fulfilled in one word, even in this: Thou shalt love thy neighbor as thyself."

- 1 John 3:11, 16-17—"This is the message that ye heard from the beginning, that we should love one another. . . . By this perceive we the love of God, because he laid down his life for us; and we ought to lay down our lives for the brethren. But whosoever hath this world's good, and seeth his brother have need, and shutteth up his compassions from him, how dwelleth the love of God in him?"

3

Widows in the Church—Part 3

Outline

Introduction

Review
I.   The Church's Obligation to Support Widows (v. 3)
II. The Church's Obligation to Evaluate Their Needs (vv. 4-8)

Lesson
III. The Church's Obligation to Maintain a High Standard for
     Widows Who Serve in the Church (vv. 9-10)
     A. They Are to Be Mature (v. 9a)
     B. They Are to Be Pure (v. 9b)
     C. They Are to Be Reputable (v.10)
        1. For being godly mothers (v. 10b)
        2. For being hospitable (v. 10c)
        3. For being humble (v. 10d)
        4. For being unselfish (v. 10e)
        5. For being kind (v. 10f)

Conclusion

Introduction

It's God's design that a husband care for his wife. She can then
be free to fulfill her biblical duties of serving her family and the
Lord. First Peter 3:7 instructs the Christian husband to "live with

[his wife] in an understanding way, as with a weaker vessel, since she is a woman" (NASB*). The implication of "weaker vessel" is that a husband is to protect, provide, and care for his wife. A wife should have the character of "a gentle and quiet spirit" and be submissive to her own husband (1 Pet. 3:4-5, NASB).

First Corinthians 7 speaks of a woman who was not married and was under her father's protection (vv. 36-38). Apparently the father wanted his daughter to be completely devoted to the Lord and not marry anyone. But Paul stated that if later in life the daughter wanted to marry, it was not sin for the father to permit her to do so. He was not bound to his original vow. The passage shows that a father is responsible to make decisions protecting his daughter's welfare. Today, we see that protection most commonly displayed when a father gives someone permission to marry his daughter.

However, a widow often has no one to protect her. That is why she is the special object of God's compassion and protection. Since the church is to demonstrate that same compassion, Paul left some guidelines so we can render proper care to widows.

Review

I. THE CHURCH'S OBLIGATION TO SUPPORT WIDOWS (v. 3; see pp. 11-14)

II. THE CHURCH'S OBLIGATION TO EVALUATE THEIR NEEDS (vv. 4-8; see pp. 14-15, 21-26)

---

*New American Standard Bible.

III. THE CHURCH'S OBLIGATION TO MAINTAIN A HIGH
STANDARD FOR WIDOWS WHO SERVE IN THE CHURCH
(vv. 9-10)

"Let not a widow be taken into the number under sixty
years old, having been the wife of one man, well reported
of for good works, if she hath brought up children, if she
hath lodged strangers, if she hath washed the saints' feet, if
she hath relieved the afflicted, if she hath diligently followed
every good work."

We know the early church had elders, deacons, and dea-
conesses (1 Tim. 3:1-13). Apparently a group of godly widows
were also given official status as servants in the church. They
were older women primarily responsible for serving the
younger women of the church. As there are qualifications
for elders and deacons, so also there are some for these
church widows. That there are qualifications for them
supports the idea that they were serving in some kind of an
official capacity. The early church kept lists of such women.

Their areas of service likely included visiting the church's
younger women to provide teaching and counseling, visiting
the sick and afflicted, and providing hospitality to travelers
such as itinerant preachers and evangelists. They probably
had a ministry to children as well. In those days, children
were often left in the marketplace because their parents
didn't want them. Abandoned boys were often trained to
become gladiators so they could eventually fight in an arena
against men or wild beasts as entertainment for the Roman
crowds. Abandoned girls were taken into brothels and used
as prostitutes. It is likely those widows found such abandoned children and placed them in good homes so they
could receive proper care.

If today's church had a group of godly widows with the
same preoccupation, its younger women would greatly
benefit. God wants those kind of widows to be active in the
church, not retire from it. Many view retirement as a time
of self-indulgence, but Scripture points toward ministry. Titus
2 says older women should have a behavior that "becometh

holiness, not false accusers, not given to much wine, teachers of good things, that they may teach the young women to be sober-minded, to love their husbands, to love their children, to be discreet, [pure], keepers at home, good, obedient to their own husbands, that the Word of God be not blasphemed" (vv. 3-5). Spiritual enrichment needs to pass from one generation to the next.

A. They Are to Be Mature (v. 9a)

"Let not a widow be taken into the number under sixty years old."

There is no evidence that the church leaders ordained those on the widow list or that the church financially supported them. *The issue of financial support stops at the end of verse 8, and the issue of qualifications begins in verse 9.* Therefore verse 9 is not saying a widow has to be at least sixty to receive financial support from the church. There is no age limit for that.

Rather, this verse is saying a widow was to be at least sixty years old to be listed as an official church helper. In many cultures it is common to associate that age with maturity. In the eastern world, sixty was the age to retire from activity and engage in a life of philosophical contemplation. In the Roman Empire, sixty was the recognized age for someone who was old. And for the widow, that age exemplified maturity.

Because of her age, it is unlikely she would want to remarry. She would be content in her present state and be drawn to a strong relationship with the Lord. She is willing to say, "Lord, I'll give the rest of my life to You."

But a widow under sixty years is more likely to consider remarriage. If she were already on the list and wanted to marry, she would be discontent in her ministry. And that discontentment could lead her to compromise her faithfulness to the Lord. Then she would bring reproach not only to herself but also to the church's testimony. Paul therefore concluded it was best that a younger widow not be placed on the list (v. 11).

B. They Are to Be Pure (v. 9b)

"Having been the wife of one man."

This literally refers to a "one-man woman." First Timothy 3 uses the same type of word construction in describing elders and deacons. It obviously doesn't refer to a woman who was married once because 1 Timothy 5:14 says it is best if younger widows remarry. And 1 Corinthians 7:39 says a widow may "marry whom she will, only in the Lord." Rather, it emphasizes a total devotion to her husband. She lived in complete fidelity to her husband, and their marriage relationship had no blemishes.

C. They Are to Be Reputable (v. 10)

"Well reported of for good works, if she hath brought up children, if she hath lodged strangers, if she hath washed the saints' feet, if she hath relieved the afflicted, if she hath diligently followed every good work."

"Good" signifies nobility and excellence of character. It is similar to the quality of blamelessness, which describes an elder and deacon (3:2, 10). She is well known for her excellent character. Verse 10 says, "She hath diligently followed every good work." She has an unrelenting pursuit of doing good to others.

There are five specific ways that she demonstrates her excellence. They give a profile of a godly woman in the same way Proverbs 31 does. Her character serves as a model not only for the younger women but also for all the women in the church. It is the kind of character that God exalts.

1. For being godly mothers (v. 10b)

"She hath brought up children."

Her children had the spiritual benefit of her godly influence. They received nourishment in a spiritual environment. Being a mother is one of the greatest privileges a woman can have because her influence will greatly affect her children's character. That doesn't mean a woman without children is less valuable to God. His plan and design for her is equally important. In fact 1 Corinthians 7 exalts a single person because he or she can be devoted to the Lord without the cares of the world. But bringing up children is the norm for most women. And the mother who lives in "faith and love and holiness with sobriety" (1 Tim. 2:15) is a model that other women should imitate.

2. For being hospitable (v. 10c)

"She hath lodged strangers."

"Lodged strangers" refers to housing missionaries, itinerant evangelists, preachers, and other Christians who were constantly traveling. Often they sought refuge from their persecutors. So it was a vital ministry to provide them with shelter. The Bible's commendation of Phoebe as a "a helper of many" undoubtedly included her aid toward traveling believers (Rom. 16:1-2). Free from the responsibilities and duties of caring for her husband and children, an older widow could devote more time and effort to that kind of ministry.

3. For being humble (v. 10d)

"She hath washed the saints' feet."

In those days, all the roads were either dusty or muddy. So people had their feet washed when coming into a home. It was a menial task that was often given to slaves. The phrase doesn't mean the widow always washed the feet of others, because she may have had a servant in the house do it as well. Rather, the phrase came to describe humility: The Christian is willing to do lowly service for the benefit of another.

Jesus was the perfect example of humility. When He washed the disciples' feet, He said, "Do as I have done to you" (John 13:15). When we see a person in need, we should help that person, no matter how lowly the task. Be willing to be inconvenienced.

4. For being unselfish (v. 10*e*)

"She hath relieved the afflicted."

"Afflicted" speaks of being under pressure, whether mental, physical, or emotional. She relieves the pressure of believers. "Relieved" (*epērkesev*) appears only here and in verse 16. Its use in verse 16 indicates support, which might include money, meals, housing, or counsel to ease the pressures of believers. Her time is spent on others, not herself.

5. For being kind (v. 10*f*)

"She hath diligently followed every good work."

This widow is like Dorcas in Acts 9. When Dorcas died, widows were "weeping and showing the coats and garments which Dorcas made, while she was with them" (v. 39). Dorcas met a vital need by making clothes for widows. They wept at the loss of one who cared so much. Likewise, the widow described here is one who helps others and is kind.

The woman who lives in those ways will honor the Lord and be a model of excellence for others to imitate.

Conclusion

Ian Maclaren, the pseudonym of John Watson, a Scottish preacher of the last century, told a story about a widow in his congregation. He visited her in the little cottage where she lived. As they were talking, she began to weep. Dr. Maclaren asked what was disturbing her. She said that when she was a girl, she surrendered her life to the Lord. And now that she was older, she sometimes thought she had done little for Him. The thought made her heart very heavy. Maclaren asked her what she had done during her life. Washing dishes, cooking meals, mopping floors, mending clothes, and rearing children was her reply.

Maclaren sat back in his chair and asked where her sons were. She replied that she named her sons after the gospel books.

Mark was a missionary in China, and Luke ministered at a mission station in Africa. Matthew served with his brother in China. And John, who was only nineteen, wanted to be a missionary in Africa with his brother. Presently he was caring for his mother since she was close to being with the Lord.

Maclaren responded that he wanted to see her heavenly reward. It would surely be great.

Focusing on the Facts

1. Why is a widow the special object of God's compassion and protection (see p. 32)?
2. What are some ways widows can serve in the church (see p. 33)?
3. What does Titus 2 teach about the behavior of older women (see pp. 33-34)?
4. True or false: There is no evidence that the church financially supported widows on the list (see p. 34).
5. What is the difference in issue between verses 8 and 9 (see p. 34)?
6. What is the significance of the age of sixty as a qualification (1 Tim. 3:9; see p. 34)?
7. What does "the wife of one man" mean (1 Tim. 3:9; see p. 35)?
8. What does "good works" tell you about the godly widow's character (1 Tim. 3:10; see p. 35)?
9. First Timothy 3:10 is similar to what chapter in Proverbs (see p. 35)?
10. What specific importance is there in being a godly mother (v. 10; see pp. 35-36)?
11. In what way did a widow show hospitality (see p. 36)?
12. What is the spiritual significance of washing the feet of believers (p. 36)?
13. Explain what relieving the afflicted means (1 Tim. 3:10; see p. 37).
14. How did Dorcas demonstrate kindness (Acts 9:39; see p. 37)?
15. In what valuable way did the widow who lived in a cottage serve the Lord (see pp. 37-38)?

Pondering the Principles

1. A widow who washed the feet of the saints demonstrated humility (1 Tim. 5:10). The Puritan John Flavel wrote, "When the corn is nearly ripe it bows the head and stoops lower than when it is green. When the people of God are near ripe for heaven, they grow more humble and self-denying. . . . Paul had one foot in heaven when he called himself the chiefest of sinners and the least of the saints" (*The Golden Treasury of Puritan Quotations*, I. D. E. Thomas, ed. [Edinburgh: The banner of Truth Trust, 1989], p. 147). Are you allowing the Lord to develop within you an awareness of your own sins and a desire to overcome them, coupled with a greater appreciation for His forgiveness? Such an outlook will help you "esteem others better than [yourself]" (Phil. 2:3).

2. The age of sixty was a point of reference to indicate maturity (1 Tim. 5:9). Spiritual maturity is the process of God's conforming the believer to the likeness of His Son. Paul expressed his desire to be like Christ when he said, "I press toward the mark for the prize of the high calling of God in Christ Jesus" (Phil. 3:14). Pressing toward the mark includes prayer (Phil. 4:6-7). Read Colossians 1:9-11 and learn how Paul prayed. Study similar passages as a guideline to teach you how to pray and be further along the path of spiritual maturity.

3. A widow who serves the church must have a holy life (1 Tim. 3:9). Read Genesis 39 to see the holiness in Joseph's life. How was Joseph tempted (v. 7)? What was his response (vv. 8-12)? Who was the focus of his attention (v. 9)? Because Joseph refused to sin, what was the outcome (vv. 21-23; cf. 41:38-44)? When you face temptation, what does 1 Corinthians 10:13 teach you?

4. The widow serving the church relieved mental, physical, and emotional pressures that believers faced (1 Tim. 5:10). To the afflicted who found relief, she was a true friend. The Puritan George Downame said, "Our afflictions are profitable, as they pluck from us false-hearted parasites, who, like the ivy, cling about us, to suck our sap, and to make themselves fat with our spoil; and to discover to us our true

39

friends, who are hardly discerned from the other till this time of trial. . . . 'A friend cannot be known in prosperity, and an enemy cannot be hidden in adversity'" (*The Golden Treasury of Puritan Quotations*, p. 113). The Bible says, "A friend loveth at all times, and a brother is born for adversity" (Prov. 17:17). Be that kind of friend to your brothers and sisters in Christ.

4

Widows in the Church—Part 4

Outline

Introduction
A. The Physical Weakness of Women
B. The Reasons for Singleness
  1. A divine calling
  2. A divine chastening
  3. A divine enrichment

Review
I. The Church's Obligation to Support Widows (v. 3)
II. The Church's Obligation to Evaluate Their Needs (vv. 4-8)
III. The Church's Obligation to Maintain a High Standard for Widows Who Serve in the Church (vv. 9-10)

Lesson
IV. The Church's Obligation to Instruct Young Widows to Remarry (vv. 11-15)
  A. So They Don't Become Frustrated (vv. 11-12)
    1. About remarriage
    2. About the Lord
  B. So They Don't Become Idle (v. 13)
  C. So They Fulfill Their Responsibilities (vv. 14-15)
    1. Of remarrying (v. 14a)
    2. Of having children (v. 14b)
    3. Of managing the home (v. 14c)
    4. Of maintaining a godly testimony (vv. 14d-15)

V. The Church's Obligation to Make Sure Capable Women Support Their Widows (v. 16)

Conclusion

Introduction

A. The Physical Weakness of Women

Because God designed a woman as the "weaker vessel," she is to receive protection and care from a man (1 Pet. 3:7). In marriage, that care comes from her husband. Before marriage, she often can find that protection from her father. "Weaker" doesn't mean weaker spiritually or intellectually, but physically. Scripture indicates women are weaker in that way.

1. Isaiah 19:16—"In that day shall Egypt be like women; and it shall be afraid and fear because of the shaking of the hand of the Lord of hosts, which he shaketh over it." Egypt was compared to women because it was a vulnerable and unprotected nation.

2. Jeremiah 50:37—"They shall become like women; a sword is upon her treasuries, and they shall be robbed." God was prophesying that when He moved against Babylon, its weakness would be like that of a woman's.

3. Jeremiah 51:30—"The mighty men of Babylon have [ceased] to fight, they have remained in their strongholds; their might hath failed, they became like women; they have burned her dwelling places; her bars are broken." Babylon's army was compared to women because it was afraid, without strength, and defenseless.

4. Nahum 3:13—"Behold, thy people in the midst of thee are women; the gates of thy land shall be set wide open unto thine enemies; the fire shall devour thy bars." The inhabitants of Ninevah were said to

be like women because they were defenseless and vulnerable to the enemy's attack.

It's not a negative thing for a woman to be a weaker vessel. In making the man stronger, God designed a wonderful partnership between him and the woman.

B. The Reasons for Singleness

However, some women never marry and experience a husband's protection. There are several possible reasons for their singleness.

1. A divine calling

It is God's plan that some believers never marry. First Corinthians 7:26-35 realistically points out that believers undergoing persecution had an advantage in remaining single. The early Christians lived in a hostile environment where they were arrested, beaten, and even killed. A married person had the added burden of caring for his wife, family, and household. If he were killed, his family probably would have had no means of support. First Corinthians 7 also implies that God gives singleness as a gift to some men and women so they can concentrate on serving Jesus Christ, without being encumbered by the cares of the world (vv. 7, 17, 28).

2. A divine chastening

Some believers might be single because they are living in disobedience to the Lord. Marriage is "the grace of life" (1 Pet. 3:7), but when we're disobedient we can expect chastening rather than blessing (Heb. 12:6-11).

3. A divine enrichment

Sometimes the Lord chooses to spiritually enrich believers during the time of their singleness. Until the single believer finds the right one for a mate, God uses the time to accomplish His divine purposes.

God's general design is that most women will marry and receive protection and provision from their husbands. However, when women in the church lose their husbands, the church needs to care for them in the proper way. So Paul instructed the church about its obligations in that area.

Review

I. THE CHURCH'S OBLIGATION TO SUPPORT WIDOWS (v. 3; see pp. 11-14)

II. THE CHURCH'S OBLIGATION TO EVALUATE THEIR NEEDS (vv. 4-8; see pp. 14-15, 21-26)

III. THE CHURCH'S OBLIGATION TO MAINTAIN A HIGH STANDARD FOR WIDOWS WHO SERVE IN THE CHURCH (vv. 9-10; see 33-37)

Lesson

IV. THE CHURCH'S OBLIGATION TO INSTRUCT YOUNG WIDOWS TO REMARRY (vv. 11-15)

"The younger widows refuse [to put on the official list]; for when they have begun to grow wanton against Christ, they will marry, having condemnation, because they have cast off their first faith. And, besides, they learn to be idle, wandering about from house to house; and not only idle but tattlers also, and busybodies, speaking things which they ought not. I will, therefore, that the younger women marry, bear children, rule the house, give no occasion to the adversary to speak reproachfully. For some are already turned aside after Satan. If any man or woman that believeth have widows, let them relieve them, and let not the church be charged, that it may relieve them that are widows indeed."

Widows in the Biblical Sense and Their Right

1. Those whose unsaved husbands desert them

   Sometimes an unbelieving husband will leave his wife when she becomes a believer. In the early church desertion was a common occurrence. First Corinthians 7:15 says, "If the unbelieving depart, let him depart. A brother or a sister is not in bondage in such cases." If an unbeliever ends his marriage with his believing wife, the woman has the privilege and right to remarry—but only a believer (7:39; 9:5).

2. Those whose husbands engage in an adulterous lifestyle

   According to the Lord Jesus, sexual sin is legitimate grounds for divorce (Matt. 5:32; 19:9), especially an ongoing adulterous lifestyle without repentance. In Old Testament times it resulted in the guilty party's death—and death certainly dissolved a marriage! God's graciousness doesn't sentence the innocent party to lifelong celibacy. Where biblical grounds for divorce exist, there is freedom to remarry.

3. Those whose husbands die

   Romans 7:2-3 says that when death dissolves a marriage there is freedom to remarry.

"I will" in 1 Timothy 5:14 speaks of calculated, rational thinking, not emotion. Paul instructed the church to encourage younger widows to remarry rather than placing them on the official list of the church's servants or helpers. Placing younger widows on the list might end up spiritually hurting them. For example, suppose an unsaved husband left his wife because she was a believer. Or perhaps she divorced him because of his ongoing adulterous lifestyle. She essentially becomes a widow, feeling hurt and brokenhearted. In the emotion of the moment she says, "I'll never marry again. I'll devote the rest of my days to the Lord. Please place me on the list so I can serve with the other godly women."

Since it could be difficult for her to sustain the commitment she made in her time of grieving, the church was to "refuse" to place her on the list (v. 11). "Refuse" is a strong word

Paul previously used in 1 Timothy 4:7: "Refuse profane and old wives' fables." The church's refusal to place younger widows on the list is an affirmation of not placing a widow on the list who is under sixty years of age (1 Tim. 5:9). However, needy widows of any age are eligible to receive financial support (vv. 3, 5). First Timothy 5:11-15 gives several reasons for the church's encouraging younger widows to remarry rather than placing them on its list of servants.

A. So They Don't Become Frustrated (vv. 11-12)

"When they have begun to grow wanton against Christ, they will marry, having condemnation, because they have cast off their first faith."

1. About remarriage

The verb "will" stresses a desire (v. 11). It's describing a woman who made a rash vow to God never to marry again, but now longs to remarry.

"To grow wanton against" means "to feel the impulses of sexual desire." It refers to a woman's desire for a man and all that entails. It's the only verse in the New Testament where the word is found. Outside of Scripture it's used of an ox trying to escape from the yoke. The picture is of a widow who wants to break out of her rash vow.

"Wanton" also implies a disregard for what is right. Unfulfilled and unhappy, she might be vulnerable to men whom she should not approach. At the same time, she knows it's wrong to break a promise. Having strong desires to remarry but feeling bound to her vow leaves her with no desire for serving in the church. In such a state she could easily compromise her Christian values.

2. About the Lord

Resenting her vow, her frustration could lead to anger against the Lord. The meaning of casting off one's first faith depends on the translation of *pistin*. If we translate it "faith," it means she abandoned her original commitment to obey, love, and serve Christ. It would be like saying, "I'm through with serving Christ, and I'm going to do what I want." If it is translated "pledge," she is saying she no longer will be subject to the vow she made to serve the Lord in the church. Either way, she's violating her commitment to the Lord.

B. So They Don't Become Idle (v. 13)

"They learn to be idle, wandering about from house to house; and not only idle but tattlers also, and busybodies, speaking things which they ought not."

A younger widow who went from home to home, instructing and counseling other church women, collected a large amount of information about the women's personal lives. But if she no longer wanted to serve others, she would accomplish little or no spiritual work.

Paul was concerned that what was originally a commitment to the Lord might turn into a social outing. The information such women collected from counseling other women could lead them to say things they shouldn't say. The Greek term "tattlers" speaks of gossip or babble. Such women speak nonsense, making empty charges and accusing by malicious words. They go from one place to the next, destroying God's people and work. That would be disastrous! "Busybodies," consumed by curiosity, look into things that aren't their concern.

There were women like that in the Ephesian church. That's one of the reasons Paul said, "I permit not a woman to teach, not to usurp authority over the man" (1 Tim. 2:12). False teaching in the church can come from women as well as men (cf. 1 Tim. 4:1). And moral and doctrinal error can result from frustrated women longing to remarry.

C. So They Fulfill Their Responsibilities (vv. 14-15)

"I will, therefore, that the younger women marry, bear children, rule the house, give no occasion to the adversary to speak reproachfully. For some are already turned aside after Satan."

Rather than placing themselves in a vulnerable position by being on the church's list, younger widows were to find fulfillment through certain areas of responsibility instead.

1. Of remarrying (v. 14a)

"I will . . . that the younger women marry."

"Younger" is a general term that doesn't specify an exact age group. Certainly it included widows at childbearing age. The church was to instruct a younger widow to remarry so she wouldn't have to struggle with her strong desires for remarriage. A husband would give her the affection, care, and provision she needed. The church's instruction reflects our Lord's compassion in caring for widows. Paul was not saying that every young woman who loses her husband is looking for trouble or is a gossip. Obviously there are exceptions.

Those who say the Bible justifies divorce but not remarriage need to explain how the church will care for its widows. When there is divorce because of the unsaved spouse's adulterous lifestyle (Matt. 5:32; 19:9) or because the unsaved spouse leaves his believing mate (1 Cor. 7:15), the Christian has the biblical right to remarry.

2. Of having children (v. 14b)

"Bear children."

Bearing children is God's purpose for most women. Losing a husband and remarrying doesn't change that. Rearing godly seed in a Christian home is God's general design for women.

3. Of managing the home (v. 14c)

"Rule the house."

This includes managing the household and nurturing the children in a Christian atmosphere. The wife and mother is to be a keeper at home (Titus 2:5), which speaks of managing the home with the resources provided. The husband provides the resources and brings them home, and the wife manages or dispenses those resources on behalf of the family.

4. Of maintaining a godly testimony (vv. 14d-15)

"Give no occasion to the adversary to speak reproachfully. For some are already turned aside after Satan."

"Occasion" speaks of a launching point or a base of operations. "Adversary" refers to any enemy of the gospel. Our ultimate enemy is Satan, but his slander usually comes through human agents. Younger widows who remarry, rear godly children, and properly manage the household give no cause for criticism against the church. But men and women who violate God's purposes give grounds for criticism.

Some people constantly criticize the church. They're Satan's instruments, looking for any fault they can find. To keep them from having any source of slander, it's best for most younger widows to remarry. That way, a woman won't be as vulnerable to sin against Christ or be lured by worldliness. Instead, she will find security, strength, and protection in a godly relationship with her husband.

Some in the church had already turned from following Christ. They listened to false teachers, acted according to their lusts, spread lies, and behaved as busybodies (2 Tim. 3:6-7; 1 Tim. 5:13).

IV. THE CHURCH'S OBLIGATION TO MAKE SURE CAPABLE WOMEN SUPPORT THEIR WIDOWS (v. 16)

"If any woman who is a believer has dependent widows, let her assist them, and let not the church be burdened, so that it may assist those who are widows indeed" (NASB).

Competent women within the church should support any widows in their fold so that the widows aren't left for the church's care. Widows' support should first come from their families (1 Tim. 5:4). If widows didn't have families to provide support, the church's men should care for them (1 Tim. 5:8). The third line of responsibility for support fell on capable women in the church (1 Tim. 5:16). Some of the capable women might have included widows themselves. And some might have been married to unbelievers. Their support didn't always have to be money—it could be meals, lodging, clothing, and many other things.

Only after those three lines of responsibility have been exhausted should the organized church provide support for its godly widows. But remember, you and I are the church. If we have the resources as individuals to support widows, we should do so. If we don't, the church should support them collectively.

Conclusion

Caring for widows should be a joy because it's our Lord's joy too! Deuteronomy 27:19 says, "Cursed is the man who withholds justice from the . . . widow" (NIV). Deuteronomy 14:29 says, "The widow, who [is] within thy gates, shall come, and shall eat and be satisfied; that the Lord thy God may bless thee in all the work of thine hand which thou doest." Since God was displeased with a lack of care for widows in Old Testament times, He certainly is displeased with a lack of care now. And since God cared for widows in those days, He certainly cares for them now!

Focusing on the Facts

1. In what sense are women "weaker" (1 Pet. 3:7)? Support your answer with Scripture (see pp. 42-43).
2. Why do some women remain single (see p. 43)?
3. Describe widows in the biblical sense (see p. 45).
4. Explain how a widow might change her thinking about remarriage (1 Tim. 5:11; see p. 46).

5. Explain how a widow might change her thinking about the Lord (1 Tim. 5:12; see pp. 46-47).
6. In what sense could a younger widow become idle (1 Tim. 5:13; see p. 47)?
7. How do younger widows benefit from remarriage (1 Tim. 5:14-15; see p. 48)?
8. Can a divorced believer remarry? Support your answer with Scripture (see p. 48).
9. Explain what it means to "rule the house" (1 Tim. 5:14; see pp. 48-49).
10. What specific benefit is there for a younger widow to maintain a godly testimony (1 Tim. 5:14-15; see p. 49)?
11. What are the four lines of responsibility in caring for widows? Support your answer with Scripture (see p. 49).
12. Why should caring for widows be a joy for every believer (see p. 50)?

Pondering the Principles

1. First Timothy 5:13 indicates that believers can act immaturely through sins such as laziness or gossip. The Puritan Thomas Brooks wrote "that sin will usher in the greatest and the saddest losses that can be upon our souls. It will usher in the loss of that divine favour that is better than life, and the loss of that peace that passeth understanding, and the loss of those divine influences by which the soul hath been refreshed, quickened, raised, strengthened, and [made glad], and the loss of many outward desirable mercies, which otherwise the soul might have enjoyed" (*Precious Remedies Against Satan's Devices* [Edinburgh: The Banner of Truth Trust, 1987], pp. 32-33). Meditate on 1 Peter 1:14-19 and allow the Spirit to increase your desire for holy living.

2. Paul wrote that some in the church were already following Satan (1 Tim. 5:15). Their lives showed a disloyalty to Christ. In contrast, three men in the Old Testament were noted for their loyalty to the Lord. King Nebuchadnezzar of Babylon ordered Daniel's friends Shadrach, Meshach, and Abednego to be thrown into a fiery furnace because they refused to worship a golden image (Dan. 3:1-30). Second Corinthians 13:5 says, "Test yourselves to see if you are in the faith; examine yourselves! Or do you not recognize this about

yourselves, that Jesus Christ is in you—unless indeed you fail the test?" (NASB). Does your life show that you are a Christian? If it does, ask the Lord to help you have the same loyalty to the Lord that Daniel's friends had.

Scripture Index

Topical Index